"[Kooser] is one of our best poets, and not simply because his style widens the reach of the art form."
—*National Review*

"Reading Ted Kooser's poetry is like wearing a favorite pair of gloves. They are so warm and comforting that you cannot weather the world without them."
—*New York Journal of Books*

"[Kooser] must be the most accessible and enjoyable major poet in America. His lines are so clear and simple."
—*Washington Post*

"[Kooser] will one day rank alongside of Edgar Lee Masters, Robert Frost, and William Carlos Williams."
—Minneapolis *Star-Tribune*

"Ted Kooser is an American original whose work in poetry is akin to the paintings of Grant Wood and the music of Aaron Copland."
—*Kenyon Review*

COTTON CANDY

COTTON

CANDY

*Poems Dipped
Out of the Air*

TED KOOSER

University of Nebraska Press   LINCOLN

Acknowledgments for the use of copyrighted
material appear on page xi, which constitutes
an extension of the copyright page.

The University of Nebraska Press is part of a land-
grant institution with campuses and programs on the
past, present, and future homelands of the Pawnee,
Ponca, Otoe-Missouria, Omaha, Dakota, Lakota, Kaw,
Cheyenne, and Arapaho Peoples, as well as those of the
relocated Ho-Chunk, Sac and Fox, and Iowa Peoples.

Library of Congress Cataloging-in-Publication Data
Names: Kooser, Ted, author.
Title: Cotton candy: poems dipped out of the air / Ted Kooser.
Description: Lincoln: University of Nebraska Press, [2022]
Identifiers: LCCN 2022003914 | ISBN
9781496231291 (paperback) | ISBN 9781496233516
(epub) | ISBN 9781496233523 (pdf)
Subjects: BISAC: POETRY / American /
General | LCGFT: Poetry.
Classification: LCC PS3561.O6 C68 2022 |
DDC 811/.54—dc23/eng/20220128
LC record available at https://lccn.loc.gov/2022003914

Set and designed in Alda by N. Putens.

To the memory of Ruth Rosekrans Hoffman,
who delighted us all.

As a writing man, or secretary, I have always felt charged with the safekeeping of all unexpected items of worldly or unworldly enchantment, as though I might be held personally responsible if even a small one were to be lost.
—E. B. White, foreword to *Essays of E. B. White*

Contents

II

III

IV

Acknowledgments

Some of these poems were previously published and are here reprinted by permission:

"Cotton Candy" in *Valley Voices*

"Dandelion," "Easter Morning," and "A Dervish of Leaves" in *How to Love the World: Poems of Gratitude and Hope* (Storey Publishing)

"A New Moon" in *Ibbetson Street*

"A Falling Feather" in *New Letters*

"Raindrop" and "A Light Snow in Late March" in *Terrain*

"Bucket" and "A Few Things in Their Places" in *Split Rock Review*

"A Brief Shower" in *James Dickey Review*

"Harpist" in *Marshmallow Clouds* (Candlewick Press)

My special thanks to Katie Schmid Henson, whose help was invaluable in selecting these poems.

A Word from the Author

My subtitle, *Poems Dipped Out of the Air*, describes the manner in which I've written these poems, a daily routine of getting up long before dawn, sitting with coffee, pen, and notebook, and writing whatever drifts into my mind. Whether those words and images are serious or just plain silly, I try not to censor myself. My objective is to catch whatever comes to me, to snatch it out of the air in words, rhythms, and cadences, the way a cotton candy vendor dips an airy puff out of a cloud of spun sugar and hands it to his customer, who in this instance is you. These poems were written in play and meant to be played with, you and I sharing them, playing together.

COTTON CANDY

Cotton Candy

The vendor, wearing a white cotton apron,
would select one paper cone from a big bouquet
of identical cones kept ready in a bucket
at hand, and, with a grand flourish, dip it
and sweep it deep in the whirling pink strands
of warm sugar, and twirl it, this with the fingers
of just one of his hands, his other hand held
out of sight, its back pressed to a bow in the ties
of his apron, and while we looked on with
delight, he would assemble a cloud, one cloud
for each of us standing in line with our quarters,
one quarter per puff of sticky, spun sweetness,
something to carry away up the midway, held
by its cone, as if we were pinching the strings
of small pink balloons that were carrying us.

Spider

Sitting with nothing to do, my knees crossed,
waggling a foot in the air, I played a game
with a tiny black spider, quick on its feet,

like an umbrella blown skittering in
from the side. It wanted to rest in the shade
of my shoe, a sizeable cloud to be under,

and when I would move it, the spider would run
to get under again. We did this a long time,
until it got angry or bored, then hopped back

out onto the light and quickly blew away
over the floor toward a potted geranium,
the tips of its spokes scarcely touching at all.

A Windy January Morning

A whirl of cold, which otherwise
would be invisible, has wrapped itself
in snow and leaves and is making
a show of toe-dancing under the light
on the porch, then scampering off into
the dark, only to prance back again.
Or are there more of them, sharing
the same costume, one under the light
while the rest huddle naked and cold
in the folds of the snow-dusty, black
velvet curtains, awaiting their turn?

Wind in the Chimney

The wind turns and turns in the chimney,
wearing her long black gown, her shawl
of February chill. She is trying
to clear the thick soot from the mirrors
using her sleeve, sighing with the effort.
From my bed I can see on the hearth
her hem stirring the ashes.

A Light Snow in Late March

There is a kind of light, thin snow
that the wind can't pick back up
once it has put it down and given it
a kick and let it unroll across
the lawn, at least a puffy wind
like this one can't, unable to
bend down far enough to get its
fingers under an edge (a fringed
edge on this morning's carpet)
to straighten it a little, although
it's making quite a show of trying,
sensing that someone may be
watching from a nearby window
where, indeed, somebody is.

Spring

Mid-March, and an empty fertilizer bag,
brown with red and black markings,
is passing through on its spring migration.

They're never in flocks, these solitary
travelers, the dull, blunt face of this one
like that of an owl, near-sighted, wings

tattered by fences from flying too close
to the freshly turned earth, inches above
its shadow as it stumbles along over

the clods, while hundreds of feet
overhead, great strings of hysterical
geese are on their way, too, crying out,

their entire civilization uprooted,
but sometimes it's trouble enough getting
from one end of a field to the other.

Turtles

Each year they appear on an early day
in spring, a line of identical turtles
who have hauled themselves out of their sleep
in the depths of the winter water, up onto

the sunny north bank of our little pond,
twenty or more, their shells shiny with chill.
They look like a row of upholstery tacks,
as if they're nailing down the muddy bank

and the hill behind it, a threadbare cushion
tweedy with browns and, here and there,
a thread of green, with a few small places
where the stuffing of snow pushes through,

but a turtle can see a very long way into
the dangers, and if you approach, plop, plop,
plop, they're right back in the winter, all
their work gone for naught, the whole hill
pulled loose along the edge of the water.

Handoff

Just a few minutes into a thunderstorm,
I saw some trees jostling each other, scrambling
for cover, and one of the ones in the lead—
there were several, shoulder to shoulder—
without slowing, turned back, and tossed
a squirrel to a tree just behind, which bent
forward—the squirrel's little legs scrabbling
for purchase—and scooped it right out
of the air, tucking it under a limb,
and they all ran on into the rain.

Culvert

It's just a rusty corrugated pipe
buried under a road with a trickle
of rainwater glinting its way down
a long ditch beside it, making a turn
toward the opening, shedding light
from its back as it enters, draping it
over a hubcap. Inside, the water
pauses and pools before moving on.
There it can hear for the first time
its own music, as if played on
a xylophone, echoing, echoing.
Haven't you heard it, that solo?
Now that I've brought you this far,
our shoes soaked by the wet grass,
and have stooped down to show you
this place where the water plays
for itself a light tune in the darkness,
you'll be able to hear it forever.

Shadows at Sunset

A soft rain of shadow is filling the ditches
that flow east from a long row of fence posts,
each shadow wider the farther they reach,
with the darkness from each blade of grass
trickling in from the edges, a million little
tributaries. Wider but shallower, too,
with the source at the foot of each post
muddy black, while far out in the pasture
the shadow's so thin and watery that you can
wade right out into it, up to your knees,
and still see your shoes on the bottom.

Clouds and Moon

I watched as thin clouds crossed the moon,
then at its fullest and brightest,
and as they approached they began to glow,
becoming more than they were
when they'd been little more than a part
of the great darkness behind them. Now they
were separate clouds, each by each
sweeping into and then out of that circle
of moonlight, perhaps circling back
when far out from the reach of the light
so as to pass through again, each of them
then sweeping away, as if dancing,
having only one moment alone with the moon,
and I saw that the hems of their gowns
brushed up dust, which for only an instant,
trailed after them into the night.

Toad

This leather bag of dimes goes hop by hop
over the highway, a motion like that of
a token in a board game, the little purse
moved forward a square at a time as if
making a bid, one toad on offer in exchange
for something of value hidden in weeds
in the opposite ditch. Could be a puddle
of silver, or another few days in this world.

Easter Morning

A misty rain pushed up against the windows
as if the house were flying through a cloud,
the drops too light, too filled with light to run,
suspended on the glass, each with the same
reflections: barn and yard and garden, grayed.

Then, suddenly appearing, burning in the quince
that soon will bloom, a cardinal, just one
milligram of red allotted to each droplet,
but each a little heavier for picking up
that splash of color, overfilled and spilling,
stumbling headlong down the chilly pane.

Burning the Prairie

There's a small puff of smoke miles away
where the sky, like a lid, has been lifted a little
by whatever's been brought to a boil.
It's a farmer who's bringing the green back,
burning thatched grass, and his smoke
lifts away, black and brown, and then whitens,
and thins, and is gone. And then there's another
in another direction, white as a milkweed seed
drifting along the blue edge, then dissolving
in light. There are times when it feels right
to be able to look at a world far away,
yet to be part of it, both feet on the ground.

———

Raindrop

I saw a raindrop, once, on the hood of a car
in a used car dealership, just that one
shining drop, but it had everything around it
in it, all of the other cars and pickups,
every red, yellow, and blue plastic pennant
flapping above it, a row of newly planted
saplings standing in line by the highway
with bandaged trunks and saggy guy-wires,
the whining traffic and the sky overhead
that was looking more and more like rain,
four or five swallows darting within it.
One drop of rain had taken in everything,
and there was my face, though a little
distorted, one flat white cheek pressed up
against that curving window, peering out
at all of the world and all that was in it,
from the inside out, for the very first time.

Bucket

I stood by the flooded Missouri,
a mile wide and varnished with light,

and a five-gallon white plastic bucket
floated past, riding deep in the water,

three or four gallons inside,
its wire handle leisurely sunning itself

on the rim, and I was delighted:
The water a bucket might carry

for decades, will, when requested to,
pick up the bucket and carry it on.

In a Glade

You have to tiptoe close to see them,
these little goldfish spots of sunlight,
glittery, swimming under the trees.
It's not as if they're looking for food
for not one rises to lip at the blue,
but, rather, they're darting this way
and that, a school of light flashing,
because, high above, a breeze paddles
around in a clumsy inflatable cloud,
playfully dabbling its fingers.

In Light from a Single Lamp

Against a bright wall, a white moth and her shadow
are dancing, fluttering into each other's embrace
and then pulling apart. With each failed attempt
she leaves dust from her wings on the surface,
though it's a dust darker than she, and could well be
from the gray, tattered wings of the shadow.
Again and again they struggle together, frustrated,
batting each other all down the wall to the floor,
where they lie for an instant, together, exhausted,
till she gathers herself, flutters up into the light,
and he follows.

Following the Weather

Today, on a country road, I found myself
driving behind the shadow of a cloud,
a mere puff of a cloud with a shadow
almost as wide as the gravel, the wind
at our backs as we both rolled south,
the shadow out a hundred yards ahead,
not raising any dust, and as I'd drive
onto the brief stretch of road that it
had passed over just a moment before,
the coolness it kept tossing out into
the ditch blew in through my windows,
fragrant with spring. It seemed to be
a stranger of a shadow, unfamiliar
with my part of the world, not knowing
to slow down on the hills, to pull over
far to the right. I kept a safe distance,
wary of what might be coming up
the other side of the day, maybe a far
darker shadow, speeding up out of
wherever we thought we were going.

Rowboat

It makes a good ear for a pond,
and it's shaped like an ear. Reach out
from the dock and set your minnow
bucket in it and the water will hear it
right to the bottom, where turtles
will lift from the mud like the heads
of automatic sprinklers and paddle
away. Then there's the thunk of your
tackle box, soon followed by the creak
of your boots on the slatted floor.
Squeaking the oars into the oar locks,
you'll never be quiet enough. Then
one good pull and you're skimming
out over what you think is a silence.
Every fish and his uncle can hear you.

In May

That morning was overcast, sprinkling rain
on a wide path of rippled, silvery light
that came toward me over a lake from a gap
in thick pines on the opposite shore.
I could see what appeared to be little fish
lipping the surface at my end of that path,
then more rings and ripples, farther away
until they were lost in the glare. I knew this
was only rain pattering onto the water,
though I couldn't see the drops, only the rings
they made, so many, too many to count,
and, delighted, I began to imagine drops
falling not down but up, from beneath that
bright path, thousands of raindrops rising
like minnows to feed on whatever lay
sprinkled over the length of that light,
having no taste for the water that lay dark
to both sides of the path, not one ripple
appearing—or which I could see—beyond
those on the light passing over the water.
I stood alone, feeling the rain on my lips,
watching thousands of silver rings spread
out and over that path, on a day right-
side-up for one moment, upside-down
for the next, back and forth, two bright
mirroring worlds with me standing
between them, trying to hold on to both.

Harpist

She has taken a great golden moth
into her arms, and with both hands
she keeps its wings pressed closed
to keep it from flying away.
And now she is drawing it closer
and smoothing the veins in its wings
as if to comfort it or give it pleasure,
and the dust that she brushes away
sprinkles into the circle of light,
tinkling as if it were music.

Dandelion

The first of a year's abundance of dandelions
is this single kernel of bright yellow
dropped on our path by the sun, sensing
that we might need some marker to help us
find our way through life, to find a path
over the snow-flattened grass that was
blade by blade unbending into green,
on a morning early in April, this happening
just at the moment I thought we were lost
and I'd stopped to look around, hoping
to see something I recognized. And there
it was, a commonplace dandelion, right
at my feet, the first to bloom, especially
yellow, as if pleased to have been the one,
chosen from all the others, to show us the way.

Yellowjacket

The weight of a single yellowjacket—
about a fifteenth of a gram—is enough
to make an overripe apple drop

from a branch, and every yellowjacket
knows to jump off those trap doors
in time, to hover nearby and watch

as the apple grows smaller and smaller,
plummeting down though a shaft of tart,
cidery air, bouncing just once, settling

into the grass with the others. Only then
does the yellowjacket follow, slowly,
as if in descending a long spiral staircase,

casually whining its way down, while
brushing the blue crystalline walls
with the fancy lace gloves of its wings.

A Brief Shower

Just an hour before dawn, not much of a storm,
more like a quarrel between two neighbors
over some ancient slight, lightning slamming doors,
then, in a moment, yanking them open again
to shout out one more curse, light splashing out
onto the sidewalks, and when at last the street
went quiet, at its far eastern end a fresh morning
was lifting the lid on the hive of it all, peering
under, wearing a hat with a veil of light rain.

The Candle's Butterfly

I waited a minute for its wings to close
before picking it up, that orange butterfly
of flame, but it died in my fingers as soon
as I pinched its wings together, and I saw
its soul escape, a delicate smoky swirl
that slowly ascended, then disappeared
into the shadows just under the ceiling.

A Kitchen Drawer

Drawers like this may hold
other worlds, but they vanish
the instant they're exposed
to the light. No one gets more
than a glimpse of what's there,
maybe a melon-ball maker
still holding a cold scoop
of light from the other side.

A Breezy Summer Morning

Nothing better to do, I sat and looked on
while young trees played in the shallow end
of the pool of the wind, splashing each other
with handfuls of leaves, the light in spatters
as they spanked and scooped it, laughing
as only trees laugh, more like a chuckle.
Such wistfulness I felt in watching them,
remembering, having once been a tree
myself, finding enough to be happy about
wherever I happened to stand.

A Thump

On a hot summer day you can hear the sun
pound once with the big heel of its hand
on the doors of a long line of boxcars at rest
on a siding, the steel cooling then warming,
thumping at random, as if to let the shadows
locked up inside know it would be foolish
to try to escape, though anyone can see
that already a few have slipped out, dropping
through cracks in the floors of the cars
on handmade ropes of darkness. If you look
you can see them behind the big wheels,
ready to run when a cloud passes by.

A Lake of Starlight

It's not just a light from above,
like a weaker moonlight, but more

like a lake in which each tree,
each person out walking alone

is suspended, all of us floating
in place like specks of dust, though

somehow passing through, which is,
of course, the manner in which

our planet is held up to the stars
by the stars. It's not a wonder

we sometimes feel buoyant,
wading out into this light.

Bicycles on Top of Cars

Often in pairs, they fly the freeways sparkling,
tethered by bungee cords. Above us
they sail on tiptoe, balanced on wobbly thin tires,
clenching their handlebars out before them
in a glitter of chromey knuckles. Through the bellow
of traffic, through fields of corn, through the mist
of mountain passes, on they fly. See the glint
of their perfect teeth, hear them trying to whistle.

Two Horses

They seem to be made of a light
like that which falls on flowing water,
and each is aware of the other's
every breath, of every ripple
rolling away from the tiny splash
of a fly, for it seems they are as one,
each a part of the other, held by
something between them
as they graze, turning and turning,
looking into each other, afloat
on a swollen, green current of meadow,
passing under the bridges of clouds.

A New Moon

A new moon, like a willow leaf,
was falling through the stars,
and as I watched, it caught on
something high above. Just then
time stopped for both of us,
moon-leaf and me below it,
as it hung there for what seemed
always in a web of constellations.
And when I felt to see if I was
still alive—it took a moment—
I looked down and saw beside
the boat I'd borrowed, drifting on
a current into time, a leaf just like
the one above, and it was moving,
too, as if to follow me along,
the water starry all around it.

A Sudden Storm

We nosed our house into a carwash of rain,
and immediately a peal of thunder jerked us
forward, and all of the lights went off and on
and off again, and a blinding downpour
rushed out of a rack of slowly rolling clouds
just as the rotary brush of our spirea bush
began to slap at the window, passing by,
then passing again, still slapping. We'd paid
with a few minutes of our day for the Deluxe
but were given an upgrade to the Ultimate,
including an underbody wash—for the cellar
got wet—and we also were entitled to a free
clear-body finish, with a glittering beading
of hail. Then, suddenly, all of the roaring
stopped, and the lights came on again,
and we could see the sun far out ahead,
and after a pause, as if taking a deep breath,
the blowers came on and we were rolled out
dripping a little, into the rest of the day.

A Walk with My Shadow

Late one afternoon, I walked a long way
following my shadow, both of us
headed east with the sun at our backs,
and the farther we walked, the harder
I found it to keep up with him, as he
stretched out his legs and strode on,
so that after a while he was gone, into
the darkening woods, and I was alone,
finding my way in pale evening light
with no shadow to follow. Then slowly
a full moon rose out of the trees
up ahead and my shadow came back
and passed me, not offering a word
of explanation, and I turned around
and followed him all the way home.

In Midsummer

Two hundred feet up, a vulture is riding
round the rim of a thermal, while beneath it
the trees try to catch at the hem of its big
shaggy shadow as it bounds through and over
their branches, soundlessly drops to the ground,
and dashes away. It looks like the vulture
is teasing the trees, the way one would play
with a kitten, trailing a feather along on
a string, and here comes that shadow again!

One Cloud

In a room with a high, vaulted ceiling,
glass all the way up into the gable,
I watched a cloud pass by four windows

of identical size, just a puff of cloud
no bigger than a hand that might dabble
the smooth blue surface of a pond

while someone else rowed, the only cloud
on an otherwise clear blue autumn morning,
drifting into, then out of the first frame,

and after a brief pause while out of sight
behind a few inches of wall, drifting over,
or onto the pane of the second window,

where I found myself moving my head
to slow it, to hold it a few moments longer
before it pulled free, disappearing before

floating out onto the third, then the fourth,
where each time I slowed it a little,
and then, as if it had never been, that cloud,

which had for a few seconds floated over
just one of my mornings, gently rippling
the glass of my windows, was gone.

Birdhouse

The rusty screw-eye had worked its way
out of the roof, and the house had dropped
through a shaft in the early summer air
like an elevator. It had struck the earth
and toppled, and had lain there days
before I picked it up—a sodden weight—
and pried it open, dug out the moldy nest
of twigs and bits of leaves and feathers,
and found three tiny, shattered eggs,
sticky with strings of yoke, and among them
dozens of ants that I'd disturbed, each with
an egg of her own, white as a grain of rice,
and no place, now, to set it down.

A Sighting

I saw an empty black plastic trash bag
hurrying along a roadside ditch
wearing no more than its flapping nightshirt,
and this on a cold day in November.

I was driving in the same direction
at about the same speed. It looked as if
it was frantic to get somewhere on time,
shouldering and pushing its way through

an invisible crowd which, as if annoyed,
shoved back, with a few of the bigger gusts
throwing punches and knocking it down
though it kept getting up, fighting for breath

and then stumbling ahead. After a while
it dropped far behind, and I sped on my way
while the bag disappeared from my mirror,
stomped flat by the boots of the wind.

A Sound in the Night

Hours before dawn I woke to the sound
of a dog far in the distance, barking,
with pauses between one bark and the next,
as if someone were pounding down nails

that had worked themselves loose in the roof
of the night and was feeling the way
nail to nail, star to star. The dog's bark
was uncertain, questioning: Was somebody

there, walking past on the Milky Way,
the footsteps like whispers, so soft in that
ancient white dust? If it were someone,
tiptoeing into forever, whoever it was

hadn't wanted to wake us, but the dog,
with the sharp, eager voice of the young,
seemed to enjoy being alive, and to love
any reason to bark at the darkness

while that person, or persons unknown,
passed the dark houses and closed gates
on the path to tomorrow, or perhaps,
came back from tomorrow, into today.

In a Shed

The head of a hammer is perched on
two ten-penny nails that it itself pounded
onto the front of the workbench, a nest
sturdy enough to bear up for a while
in the harsh wind of time, like the others
the swallows have hung on the rafters
and tucked under the eaves of the roof,
though today time's a summery breeze
making the walls squeak a little, dust
dappled with light spattering down
through the sun-riddled tin roof, dotting
the bench, two buckets, one coil of wire
and a snake snaking over the oil-blackened
floor, flicking its red tongue, tasting
the cheeps falling out of the shadows.

A Cloudy Sunrise

The sun was reluctant to get up,
probably knowing too well that the fields
would be cold underfoot. It lay there
with a cloud pulled up over its face,
under a comforter with a border
embroidered with bare trees and crows.
I put on the kettle for coffee and fried up
some Jimmy Dean sausage links, thinking
the smell would entice it, but even when
the toast popped up with its coarse
morning cough, the world stayed dim.
I could feel that the rest of the day
was losing its patience, for someone
under the ice on the river had turned on
soft fluorescent lights, so that the fish,
who'd stood in line all through the night,
could get on with delivering bubbles.

A Novelty

If you drop

the capsule
of a sleeping bat

into a glass
of sunset

it will magically

unfold.

In a Cold Late-Afternoon Rain

In a cold late afternoon rain,
a man with no shirt, wearing
a yellow Day-Glo vest, is pushing
a long, reluctant centipede
of shopping carts across
a puddled supermarket lot,
some of the carts with locked wheels,
all of them squealing or jingling
from puddle to puddle. His shoes
are wet, his head is bent, his wet hair
stringy and swinging. His bony
shoulders are blue with tattoos.
It looks as if he's pushing the rest
of his life out ahead, skinny arms
covered with goose-bumps
reaching out toward the future.

A Fluttering

Out walking the checkerboard edge of a hayfield,
stepping onto, then out of the patches of shade
from trees that leaned over a fence I was following,
I saw something ahead, at eye level, fluttering,
flashing as fast as the clicks in a bicycle chain,
and thinking that it was alive, I moved up on it
slowly. But as I grew near I could see it, a leaf,
pale yellow, caught at the end of a long strand
of all but invisible silk, let down from above,
and though it wasn't the butterfly or the moth
I'd expected, it was doing a commendable job
of mimicking life, caught up in a terrible struggle,
so I swept a hand over it, breaking the silk tie
and setting it free, though for a few steps it swung
from the cuff of my sleeve as if wanting to follow,
so, unembarrassed, nobody around, I spoke to it,
just a few words of assurance, then let it down
gently, into a shadow, and went on my way.

Melon

By the time we discovered it under the vines
it was too ripe to pick, its down side soft
and leaking bees, so we left it, a pale yellow,
partly deflated, baggy old birthday balloon,
though we reeled in the coarse nets of vine
for the compost heap. All winter that melon
bobbed like a float in the slow tides of snow,
losing its color, and by spring it was hollow,
translucent, a shell from which something
had pecked its way out and was gone
like the past, leaving a trickle of seeds.

A Falling Feather

The bird that had dropped it had already flown on
by the time I glanced up from my walk and saw it
a few yards ahead, a white feather, slowly and carefully

rocking its way, step to step, down a staircase of air
like a candle in the hand of a heavy, invisible man
who was hesitant, apparently fearful of falling,

one of his hands on a bannister, and in the other
the burning white flame of a feather as he felt his way
down into the light at the bottom. All the world

stopped to watch until at last he bent and carefully
set the flame down in the grass, where it became
only a feather, undistinguished, a creamy white

with a stain of pale yellow at the tip of the quill,
though still warm, still fluttering ever so slightly,
glowing with light that had fallen so slowly, so far.

A Few Things in Their Places

A brick on the lid of a beehive, five tires
weighing down the tarpaper roof on a shed,
close to a hundred round thousand-pound bales
holding the prairie flat all the way out
to its edge and, next to an abandoned school,
a teeter-totter pressing the tip of a finger
on something that once happened there.

A Light in a Farmyard

The night is a tarp worn thin by hard use,
thrown over the days, thousands of stars
showing through, especially where it's been
folded and folded again at the Milky Way.

One little hole in the fabric has opened
a few yards away, letting yesterday—
or is it tomorrow?—leak through, the canvas
around it so thin that it glows like a halo.

But it's only an everyday bulb at the top
of a pole, showing the pole and below it
a circle of dust. One can see hundreds
just like it all along the horizon. But is that
a horizon we see, or the hem of the night
too loosely staked to the ground?

A Seascape

In September, before the first frost,
on a wet city street where a fireman
had flushed out a hydrant, I saw dozens
of butterflies drinking, little gray boats
riding low in the water, with triangular
calico sails, each tugging its anchor,
their bows pointing into the wind.

Full Moon

Midnight, and the lake is a couple of hours
into the late shift, standing on either side

of a long conveyor belt of silver ripples,
nearly all perfect and the rest within standards,

the rollers beneath well-oiled with darkness
and altogether soundless now, though by dawn

they'll be chirping and crying, the belt slapping
a little, like wings taking off from the water.

A Dervish of Leaves

Sometimes when I'm sad, the dead leaves
in the bed of my pickup get up on their own
and start dancing. I'll be driving along,
glance up at the mirror and there they'll be,
swirling and bowing, their flying skirts
brushing the back window, not putting a hand
on the top of the cab to steady themselves,
but daringly leaning out over the box,
making fun of the fence posts we're passing
who have never left home, teasing the rocks
rolled down into the ditches, the leaves light
in their slippers, dancing around in the back
of my truck, tossing their cares to the wind,
sometimes, when I'm down in my heart.

IV

A Windy Monday

Much as a gymnast will skip a few steps
with her hands in the air, then place them
fingertips first on the floor, though for only
an instant, then flatten her whole hand

in the manner a duck puts down a foot—
but faster than that—and then jauntily
launch herself, heels over head, into
a backward somersault, then do it again,

and then, while flying upside down, turn
a full twist in the air and land hands high,
just so, this grocery insert from yesterday's
newspaper skips out of an alley—wearing

meat red and carrot yellow—drops into a roll,
jumps up again, springs from its fingertips
high over my windshield, flips once, and is
gone. This poem's a round of applause.

Egg Carton

This dull gray caterpillar was much too numb
from its days in the dark refrigerator
to be able to walk very far on its stumpy legs,
so here it sits, little more than a shell of itself,
cracked open, empty on the kitchen counter,
a bright yellow omelet having fluttered away.

Cornshucks

If you live in corn country you've seen them.
They're all on the move now, October,
blowing out of the harvested fields,
hurdling wire fences, quite a few leaping
and rolling like pole-vaulters, picking
themselves up from the ditches, scrabbling
over the gravel, out over the highways,
a few getting caught with the grasshoppers
on the grilles of the humorless grain trucks,
the rest leaping into the opposite ditches,
the grass glinting with overnight frost,
some lying down to roll under the low wire,
then springing right up, brushing the dust
from the sleeves of their raincoats
and scurrying on, leaping from furrow
to furrow, feeling terribly empty, or so
one imagines, not giving a thought to
what's coming, bewailing what's been,
a few badly hobbled, a few falling down,
a number hysterical, out of control,
waving their frostbitten hands in the air.

A Winter Landscape

As far as I can see, across the city,
quill pens of smoke are dipping their tips
into the inkwells of chimneys,
so many pens ready to write, but not one

of them writing. But just over there
is a house with no pen. The well must have
gone empty. There were probably
lots of bad stories, bleak stories, dashed off,

then crumpled and tossed to the winds.
You've seen clouds like those, pale wads
of breath at a shelter where people
wait and wait for a bus. I'd guess nothing

is left in that house with no feather
but a dusting of snow blown in under
the door, and a thin skin of dried ink
lining the walls of the chimney.

A Leaf in Wind

In a light winter wind I watched a dead leaf
tied to a twig by a short length of thin stem
behave like a bird, a red-brown wren-like bird
on one leg, with a fluttery temperament, facing
one way for a minute, then turning to peck at
the twig. It was much too cold for ants to be out
but there was apparently something quite small
just behind it, doggedly following, something
that either the leaf didn't like or that it wanted
to eat, so tiny it made for quite difficult pecking
while keeping one's balance on one leg in wind,
bobbing and weaving, with a beak little more
than a broken-off tooth at the tip of a leaf.

On a Dark Winter Morning

Is that the sound of a car's starter motor
cranking over and over again in the cold,
and then, after a few moments have passed,
trying it again? No, that's the call of an owl
from a tree somewhere out in the darkness
on a branch overhanging the snow.
It has a battery that never runs down.

Pleasures of Snow

First came a freezing mist that darkened the deck
with a brittle glaze, and soon what looked like broken rings
of snowflakes spiraled in, though slowly, a few of them
holding hands, then letting go and opening their chutes,
and floating down to lean against each other on the ice.
Then, resting there, they waited till a breeze would come
from somewhere far across the early evening dark
and take the hand of one and spin it out and away, far
to the edge of the light, and a few of the others would soon
join hands and tentatively follow.

An Oriole Nest in Winter

An oriole has left her saggy evening bag
snagged on a branch, a cheap accessory
crocheted from hay and orange baling twine
with beads of blue sunlight interwoven,
the orange to match her outfit and the blue
as an accent to pick up the sky through which
she came and went before she flew away
to join the snowbirds at their winter place
where no bird needs a fancy evening bag,
but rather, like the chickadee, a simple cap
for sitting by a birdbath with the others,
having a sip, maybe leaving a seed as a tip
for the starlings for doing such a good job
of picking things up, but all of this is
supposition. All we really have is a nest
at the end of a twig, a little like a purse
in appearance, threadbare on a winter day,
the missing eggs all spent to buy the future.

November Snow

Snow all afternoon, but lighter
at dusk, and someone has drawn,
as if in soft pencil, a barn on the side
of the distance, drawn trees, too,
and blurred them with a fingertip,
and blurred the ghost of a house
as if it stood back from the barn.
And as the snowfall lessens
and lightens and night comes on,
I see a dab of glowing yellow
on first one window, then another.

After an Ice Storm

Twenty degrees, and the clouds so far above, so thin,
that the watery light of eternity shows through.

Earlier, somebody poured something too hot in the cup
of the day, the one cup we've been given, cracking

the glaze, which now is a web of glittering twigs spread
over the bottom, though some of the cracks have risen

up the sides like trees branching. Imagine yourself small,
standing with me on the bottom, pale light from the sky

porcelain-white all around us, as glimpsed through
those trees I described, which we can hear clicking

a little as the crazing continues, twig touching twig,
a glassy sound all around us, down inside of today.

A Falling Branch

A branch in a tree outside my door
has broken away from somewhere above
and begun to fall, but a lower branch
has reached to catch it, and the two,
clinging onto each other, dance a last dance
in the wind, a springy waltz with bows
and curtsies, the strong branch teasing
the falling branch, swinging it out and over
its shadow beneath on the snow.

Fresh Snow, with Deer Tracks

Their hooves have broken through the white
into a shallow, watery blue that's flowing
into March, and they've kicked up splashes
ahead of each step that since have frozen
sandy and white on the crust. Somehow
the one out in the lead knew how to skirt
the deeper, colder blues, and you can see
by now, I hope, how all the others followed.

A Man Walking in Deep Snow

From a freshly plowed country road, a white
canal all the way to the horizon, we see him
in insulated coveralls and a cap with earflaps,
halfway between house and barn, lifting his knees,
then punching them down, his boots never quite
clearing the surface of the snow, his arms out wide
like a landing hawk, his gloves frantically grabbing
for bannisters that aren't there. It's as if he were
wading out into a flood, or trying to stomp out
a fire he's started and which now has spread out
everywhere and over everything, and though
he knows we're here, he's not waving for help.
His whole self's going to do this, all on his own,
and we speed on and into other territories.

Icicle

I watched an icicle busily gathering light
from a warming winter afternoon, but soon it
was trying to carry too much, and dropped
one little piece, and then another and another.

A Stand of Ornamental Grass

It's one of those decorator winter days
with a gray dropped ceiling, walls
tastefully painted a silvery off-white,

hung all around with empty mirrors
framed by trees, the great room of it all
lit softly from not too far above by

long fluorescent tubes in fixtures
recessed in the milky, light-diffusing
clouds, in short, a beauty salon of a day,

with a stand of ornamental grass—
soft bleached-blonde seed heads
being blow-dried—and, although

I can't make out what they're saying,
they're all talking at once, and with
great agitation, shaking their layered

shoulder-length hair, bobbing and
weaving, some of them arguing,
getting right up into each other's faces

as if shouting, as if something quite
shameful has happened, somewhere
beyond all this, off over the snow.

A Special Kind of Sunset

You, too, have seen them at times, those rare sunsets
when the light squeezes in under a low layer of clouds

and illuminates everything, but just on the west face—
cut cornstalks in snow, phone poles and fence posts—

no middle-range dimness, only gold or black shadows
reaching all the way back to the morning. What's left

of that day has paused, turned, and come back, and is
lifting the lid just a little to be sure we're still there.